Background for the Teacher

The following information is provided to highlight the unit's themes and any background knowledge or vocabulary work that may be indicated for students. Two sections, SYNOPSIS and IDEAS SUGGESTED BY THE STORY, are intended only for the teacher, as a help in anticipating issues students might raise about the story. However, students may enjoy brainstorming their *own* list of IDEAS SUGGESTED BY THE STORY as a closure activity. The final background section, RELATED BOOKS, addresses some of the themes in *Island of the Blue Dolphins* and provides a source for further reading.

Synopsis
From 1835 through 1853 a young girl named Karana grew to womanhood while living alone on an island near Santa Barbara, California. *Island of the Blue Dolphins* is Scott O'Dell's fictionalized version of her story. As the novel opens, Karana lives a hard yet pleasant life with her family on the Island of the Blue Dolphins. After a rival tribe massacres most of the men in her tribe, a ship comes to take the survivors to a safer place. Karana jumps ship when she sees that her young brother has been accidently left ashore. Almost immediately her brother is killed by wild dogs and Karana is faced with solitude and a harsh environment. Overcoming depression and despair, she learns to be resourceful. Seeking companionship, for example, she lovingly tames the most cunning of the wild dogs. Karana's respect for the natural world, her resiliency, and her courage are an inspiring tribute to human endurance and ingenuity.

Things students need to know

San Nicolas Island. This island, off the coast of Los Angeles, is the setting for *Island of the Blue Dolphins.*

Sea Hunters. At the time of this story, different tribes of sea hunters still lived along the Pacific coast and traveled for great distances to find their prey.

Aleuts. The Aleuts are natives of the Aleutian Islands, now in the state of Alaska.

Pelts. The pelts of sea animals were very valuable to white men during the 1800s.

Things students need to know *(continued)*

Gender Roles. In many societies, a clear distinction has traditionally existed between jobs for men and jobs for women.

Vocabulary development

There are many new words in this book, and two techniques will be used with vocabulary.

First, give students a list of some of the words that may cause them difficulty as they read (see the following page). Explain that some of the words they may already know, some may be familiar words used in a new way in the book, and some will be entirely new to them. If they need to know any of these words as they read, suggest strategies that all good readers use:

- Look up the word in a dictionary.

- Ask a friend.

- Try to figure out what the word means from context.

- Guess.

The second approach to vocabulary in this unit is to highlight words that will be necessary to students' understanding of the story section by section. In this Partner Unit, such words have been put into word classes (according to parts of speech) and defined with a consistent pattern like that used in "Vocabulary Charting." In *Island of the Blue Dolphins*, these words are either nouns or verbs.

There is no lesson to be "taught" here about grammar. Instead, students should recognize that grammar helps them develop systems for understanding words. They may even begin to see that they do indeed classify words in their heads as they encounter them.

Difficult Word List

A abandoned
ancestors
awl

B barb
bellowing
bolder
bound
braced

C ceased
chafing
circlet
clamor
coils
cove
crevices
crouching

D darting
deserted
disks
dodging
dunes
dusk
dyeing

F fateful
fashioned
fierce
flank
fledglings
fleshed
flippers

G gash
gnawed
gorged

H headland
herbs
herd

I idle

L lapped
lashed
launch
leagues
leeches
limp

M matted
manhood
mesa

N nettles
notched

O olivella
ornaments

P perch
planks
pitch
portioned
pursue
pursuer
prey
prowling
prying

R reeds
reefs
rejoicing
retreat
rightful
rites

S sandspit
scallops
scarce
scurrying
seeping
serpent
shaft
sheltered
shimmered
slashed
slain
sloping
slunk
smothered
snares
speckled
snared
sparingly
spouting
stale
stalks
stride
stunted
suckers

T thong
thrust
toyon

U urchins

V venturing
vowed

W warily
warriors
webbed
whined
whirled
wreath
wreckage
wriggling

ISLAND OF THE BLUE DOLPHINS : TEACHER'S GUIDE

Ideas suggested by the story

- Severe conditions often bring out capabilities we didn't know we had.

- Men and women are capable of doing similar tasks.

- Most of us long for human companionship.

- We often do courageous things to help those we love.

- Animals can be a great comfort to people.

- Nature can be harsh.

- Animals follow their instincts.

- There are good and evil people in every racial or cultural group.

- In some societies, sex roles are clearly defined.

- The more people learn about animals, the more they usually respect them.

- Even when things are stressful, we value little pleasures.

- We all possess resources of which we are unaware.

- Sometimes it is hard to know if primitive behavior is civilized and if civilized behavior is primitive.

- Almost all people enjoy beautiful things.

- Different groups have different customs.

- Humans are adaptable.

- New situations can be frightening.

- Life is particularly difficult when one must do all of the necessary work alone.

- We learn a lot about ourselves when we live alone.

Related books

George,
Jean Craighead

Julie of the Wolves *Harper & Row, 1972*
Julie and Karana both learn to trust themselves to behave with
courage and hope. Learning to survive in hostile environments, they
also learn how to tame the harsh fears that hound them.

The Talking Earth *Harper & Row, 1983*
Billie Wind, a contemporary native American, learns that we all
must listen to the land and the animals if we are to survive. Like
Karana, she discovers that we all play a part in the life of our planet.

Paulsen, Gary

Hatchet *Puffin, 1977*
Brian, like Karana, finds himself alone and afraid. Also like Karana,
he learns that he must trust and rely on himself. The need for
thoughtful and often difficult decisions helps Brian mature.

Introductory Activities

Suggestions for introducing the story

From the activities below, select one or two that are best suited for your class.

Questions to Karana. Read "Author's Note" (pages 182–184). Ask the students to generate questions they might have liked to have asked the real woman found on San Nicolas. Record the questions. Ask the students to see whether they find answers as they read the story. (After students finish the PARTNER PAGES, bring this list back out. Are some of the questions answered? Are some of the questions unanswerable? Discuss this.)

Loneliness. Read the poem "Loneliness" to the class. Have the students discuss what it would mean if the person in the poem were really and truly alone—isolated from all people. Discuss what it would mean if the person in the poem was around people but felt lonely.

Loneliness

Still, still, stillness
In my head, in my heart.
      Is there anyone there?
      Is there anyone there?
The world's outside
And I want to be a part.
      Is there anyone there?
      Is there anyone there?

There's a coldness inside,
It's so very wintery.
I'm here. Here I am,
Alone and lonely.
      Is there anyone there?
      Is there anyone there
      For me?
            —Felice Holman[1]

Introductory Activities *(continued)*

Scavenging from Nature. Take the class on a 15-minute treasure hunt around the school. Have students bring back to class any natural thing that they find—a rock, a piece of bark, a leaf, and so forth. Look over the class collection and discuss what each object might be used for. If they had to make everything they needed from natural products, what objects would students make out of the different natural materials in the collection?

Feathers. Ask the students to bring in any feathers that they might have. Talk with them about all of the things that we make from feathers. Discuss which of their feathers might be useful for different purposes.

Partner Reading

Have pairs of students read the book together and complete the PARTNER PAGES of this unit.

Connection Activities

When students have completed the book and partner activities, bring the class back together for one or two of the activities below.

Connections—for the whole class

Wonderful Words I. Write the following poem on the board or project a transparency of it. Have students read it silently or to partners, and then read it aloud to the class. Then ask:

- How do you think Karana might respond to this poem?

- Are words as wonderful when there is no one else to hear them?

The Wonderful Words

Never let a thought shrivel and die
For want of a way to say it,
For language is a wonderful game
And all of you can play it.
All that you do is match the words
To the brightest thoughts in your head
So that they come out clear and true
And handsomely groomed and fed—
For many of the loveliest things
Have never yet been said.
Words are the food and dress of thought,
They give it its body and swing,
And everyone's longing today to hear
Some fresh and beautiful thing.
But only words can free a thought
From its prison behind your eyes.
Maybe your mind is holding now
A marvelous new surprise!
—Mary O'Neill[2]

ISLAND OF THE BLUE DOLPHINS : TEACHER'S GUIDE

Connections—for small groups

Wonderful Words II. Have partners read the poem "The Wonderful Words" and then collaborate on a short speech Karana might make about something she loved.

Island Images. Have students work in small groups or with partners to recreate a scene from the book that was particularly meaningful to them. They might create murals, dioramas, or, with some costuming help, *tableaux vivants* (where human models are posed).

Preserving the Past. Remind students that Karana was the last remaining person from her tribe. Ask them to imagine being Karana and having the opportunity to go back to the island to collect things for a museum, so that later generations will know something about the culture of her tribe. Have partners discuss and list the things Karana might want to collect.

Connections—for students working individually

A Monument for Karana. Ask students to imagine being commissioned by the city of Santa Barbara to design a new monument to mark Karana's grave. Have them design this monument to communicate both who Karana was and what she might mean to people today.

Connections—for a home activity

Society's Rules. Review the earlier discussion about why a society would make a rule that forbade women from making weapons. Then tell the class that you want them to explain to a parent or another adult about both the rule and how Karana found she had to break the rule to survive. Then the student and the adult are to make a list of what society gains and loses by having rules that say what roles (or jobs) people may and may not have.

Society's Rules

Tell your parent or another adult about the men's and women's roles (jobs) in *Island of the Blue Dolphins*. Explain that it was a rule of the tribe on the island that women could not make weapons, but that Karana found she had to break the rule to survive when she was alone. Together, make a list of what society gains and loses by having rules that tell people what roles (jobs) they may and may not have.

What society gains by having rules that determine our roles:

What society loses by having rules that determine our roles:

Sign here, please!

_____

_____

After you have completed your lists, each of you please sign your name and the date. If you have any comments about the activity, write them on the back of the page. Thank you.

ISLAND OF THE BLUE DOLPHINS : HOME ACTIVITY

PARTNER PAGES

Island of the Blue Dolphins

by Scott O'Dell

Name _____

Partner's Name _____

Copyright © 1996 Developmental Studies Center

Partner Pages

You and your partner will work together throughout these pages in order to discuss ideas and questions you have about *Island of the Blue Dolphins.* You will also work together to complete the activities that follow.

Reading 1   **Read.** Chapters 1 and 2 (pages 1–14).

Word Class	Word	Big Category	Description/Uniqueness
noun	Aleut	is a person	indigenous to the Aleutian Islands, which extend south from the Alaskan peninsula.
noun	Cormorant	is a seabird	with beautiful greenish-black feathers. It is large.
noun	Kelp	is seaweed.	
verb	To parley	is to talk	together, usually when people have different sides to protect.

ISLAND OF THE BLUE DOLPHINS : PARTNER PAGES   **PP1**

Partner Activity. Discuss with your partner whether or not the people of the island should have trusted Captain Orlov. Then complete the statement(s) below, listing as many reasons for your position as you can.

circle one:
I//We   think the people of the island should trust Captain Orlov because

signed:

circle one:
I//We   think the people of the island should not trust Captain Orlov because

signed:

Reading 2   **Read.** Chapters 3 and 4 (pages 15–24).

Word Class	Word	Big Category	Description/Uniqueness
noun	Carcasses	are dead bodies,	especially of animals.
noun	Pelts	are animal skins,	usually with the fur or hair left on.

Partner Activity. Imagine that you are Captain Orlov. You have just caused the slaughter of most of the male population of this island so that you could take all of the otter pelts instead of half. Discuss with your partner how Captain Orlov might justify his and the Aleuts' behavior. With your partner, write a dialogue between Captain Orlov and a character we'll call Captain Chekhov, who is known throughout the Pacific for his fair treatment of native peoples.

Reading 3   **Read.** Chapters 5, 6, and 7 (pages 25–40).

Word Class	Word	Big Category	Description/Uniqueness
noun	Shirkers	are people	who put off doing work.
noun	Yucca	is a plant	that is tall and grows in the New World.
verb	To grumble	is to complain	to yourself, but loudly enough to be heard by others.
verb	To perish	is to die.	
verb	To ponder	is to think	carefully.

Partner Discussion. Discuss the following questions with your partner:

• Why was it a wise choice for the people of the Island of the Blue Dolphins to leave?

• How do you feel about Karana's choice to swim back to be with her brother?

Reading 4   **Read.** Chapters 8 and 9 (pages 41–58).

Word Class	Word	Big Category	Description/Uniqueness
noun	A tusk	is an animal tooth	that is long and pointed.

Partner Discussion. Have a long discussion with your partner about the two questions below. See if you can understand all of the things that Karana might be thinking. You need not write your ideas down, but talk about them as thoughtfully as you can.

• Following the death of Ramo, what are all of the thoughts in Karana's head?

• What are all of the reasons that Karana is doing as little as possible?

Partner Activity. Discuss the following question with your partner. After you have finished the discussion, collaborate on a written answer to the question.

• Why would a group make a law that forbade women from making weapons?

Reading 5   **Read.** Chapter 10 (pages 59–68).

Word Class	Word	Big Category	Description/Uniqueness
noun	An omen	is a sign	that something—good or bad—is about to happen.

Partner Discussion. Discuss the following questions with your partner:

• Why did Karana feel that she had to leave the Island of the Blue Dolphins?

• Why did Karana feel that she had to return to the Island of the Blue Dolphins?

Reading 6   **Read.** Chapters 11 and 12 (pages 69–79).

Word Class	Word	Big Category	Description/Uniqueness
noun	Bulls	are sea elephants	that are adult and male.
noun	Cows	are sea elephants	that are adult and female.
noun	Embers	are pieces of coal and wood	that are still burning in a dying fire.
noun	Gruel	is cooked cereal	that is thin and watery.
noun	Sinew	is a dried strip	of tough animal flesh—a tendon.

Partner Activity. Discuss the question below with your partner. Each of you write your own individual answer to it, then read what you have written to your partner.

• Karana says that she is happy to be home. How does her behavior make us believe her?

Reading 7   **Read.** Chapters 13 and 14 (pages 80–90).

Word Class	Word	Big Category	Description/Uniqueness
noun	A rival	is a person	who competes with another over something.

Partner Discussion. Have a long discussion with your partner about the questions below. See if you can understand all of the things that might be occurring to Karana. You need not write your ideas down, but talk about them as thoughtfully as you can.

• Why is it that Karana is becoming more clever and resourceful?

• Why is she working so much harder?

• Why is she doing "man's work"?

Reading 8   **Read.** Chapters 15 and 16 (pages 91–104).

Word Class	Word	Big Category
noun	A devilfish	is an octopus.

Partner Activity. Discuss all three of the questions below with your partner. After your discussion, each of you choose a different question to answer in writing. Read what you have written to your partner. Discuss your ideas.

• Why has Karana saved the leader of the wild dog pack rather than let him die?

• What does Karana mean when she says, "I did not know how lonely I had been until I had Rontu to talk to"? *(page 101)*

• Why did Karana and Rontu learn to trust and love each other?

Reading 9   **Read.** Chapters 17, 18, and 19 (pages 105–124).

Partner Discussion. Have a long discussion with your partner about the questions below. See if you can understand all of the things that Karana might be thinking and feeling. You need not write your ideas down, but talk about them as thoughtfully as you can.

• Why did Karana let Rontu handle the problem with the wild dog pack his own way, when she could have killed the dogs?

• Even though Karana has no other people with her, she and Rontu seem to be happy during this time. Why might this be so?

• Karana has learned how to take care of herself in a wild and lonely place. How do you think she feels about her new strengths and abilities?

PP6   *ISLAND OF THE BLUE DOLPHINS: PARTNER PAGES*

Reading 10   **Read.** Chapters 20 and 21 (pages 125–140).

Partner Discussion. Discuss the following questions with your partner:

- Why was Black Cave so scary to Karana?

- What does Karana fear with the return of the Aleuts?

- Why was Rontu not afraid of the Aleut girl?

- Why does Karana lie to the Aleut girl?

- How does Karana know that Tutok did not tell that she was on the island?

Reading 11   **Read.** Chapter 22 (pages 141–146).

Partner Discussion. Discuss the following questions with your partner:

- Why did Karana reveal herself to Tutok and trust her enough to tell Tutok her secret name?

- Even though they did not speak the same language, Tutok and Karana became real friends. Why was friendship important to both of them?

Reading 12   **Read.** Chapters 23 and 24 (pages 147–156).

Partner Activity. Discuss the question below with your partner. After you have finished the discussion, collaborate on a written answer to the question.

- Why has Karana, unlike anyone in her group before, decided not to kill the animals?

Reading 13   **Read.** Chapter 25 (pages 157–160).

Something to Think About. Think about Rontu's death. Think about what this was like for Karana. What would it have been like for you if you were in her place? What is it about the death of a beloved pet that leaves one with an empty feeling? If you wish, talk about your ideas with your partner.

Reading 14 **Read.** Chapters 26 and 27 (pages 161–170).

Partner Discussion. Discuss the following questions with your partner:

• Why did Karana want to capture and tame Rontu's son?

• Since Karana can manage in her environment so well, why would the tidal wave and earthquake be so frightening to her?

Reading 15 **Read.** Chapters 28 and 29 (pages 171–181).

Partner Activity. Discuss *all* the questions below with your partner. After your discussion, each of you choose a different question to answer in writing. On separate pieces of paper, each of you write a first draft answer to your question. Trade papers and read what your partner has written. Do you think anything needs to be added or changed? Discuss your ideas with your partner. Each of you write a second draft of your answer. Use any of your partners' suggestions that will improve your piece.

• How must Karana have felt after the first rescue boat left her?

• Why did Karana get all dressed up and paint her tribal sign and the sign of an unmarried woman on her face?

• Why was she willing to leave for an unknown place?

• Why do we long to be with other people so?

• How must Karana feel about herself for having managed to live so long on her own?

Reading 16 **Read.** Author's Note (pages 182–184).

Partner Discussion. Talk with your partner about how well you think Scott O'Dell did in taking a real event and imagining how it might have been. Would you like to know more about the real Lost Woman of San Nicolas?

PP8   *ISLAND OF THE BLUE DOLPHINS: PARTNER PAGES*

Looking back at *Island of the Blue Dolphins*

Partner Discussion, Individual Review. Talk with your partner about your opinion of this book. Write a review of it for other readers. Tell them what you liked and/or disliked about the book, and describe how *Island of the Blue Dolphins* compares with books you have especially liked. Give the book an overall rating (from 1 to 10) and justify your rating.

A Vivid Scene. Think about the scene in the book that was most vivid in your mind. Draw a picture of it. Be prepared to explain your scene to the rest of the class.

What Did She Look Like? Draw a picture of Karana as she looked when she went down to meet the men who were to take her off the Island of the Blue Dolphins. Have a class display of all the different portraits of Karana.

UNIVERSITY OF RHODE ISLAND

3 1222 01017 886 4

NO LONGER THE PROPERTY
OF THE
UNIVERSITY OF R. I. LIBRARY